THE TWO RONNIES
IN A PACKED PROGRAMME TONIGHT..

A Star Original

The Two Ronnies' dialogue is the sharpest on
television — as newscasters they are certainly
unrivalled. Now their script associate, Ian
Davidson, has made another collection of the
most outrageous and hilarious news items that
ever hit the screen. Stand by for the latest
world-shattering reports on how Raquel Welsh
caused appalling traffic congestion at London
Airport, and what happened when Telly Savalas
bent down to tie his shoe lace in a bowling
alley . . .

D1470875

All this would have been impossible — though it might have been easier — without this handful* of writers:-

Alec Adcock, Peter Bain, Alec Baron, Robert Belford, Dennis Berson, George Brodie and Mike Perry, Alex Brown and Pat Murray, Peter Campbell and Roger Ordish, Philip Campbell and Myron Edwards, Garry Chambers, Syd Clark, John Cotterill, Barry Cryer, Roy Dixon and Ken Wallis, Dave Dutton, Malcolm Drew, Pete Edwards, Paul Eldergill, Harry Evans, Eric Flitcroft, Ernest Forbes, Fuzz, Phil Gould, Stephen Hancocks, Bob Hedley, Les Higgins, Tim Hopkins, Howard Imber, John Irving, Stephen Kidd, Dorothy Kilmurry-Hall, Gary Knight, Tom Magee-Englefield, Malcolm Mather, Wally McKinley, Chris Miller, Phil Munnoch, Peter Osborne, Anthony Nicholson, Wendy Norton, Gavin Osbon, Jon Peat, Terry Ravenscroft, Keith Rawnsley and Pete Long, David Renwick, Tony Rich, Peter Robinson, Kenneth Rock, Laurie Rowley, Les Scott, Tony Stevens, John Sullivan, Terry Treloar, Peter Vincent, Len Walker, Ron Weighell, Alan Wightman.

*The hand in question is one of the Royal College of Surgeons' most prized possessions.

Also featuring the Two Ronnies' dialogue in *Star*
BUT FIRST THE NEWS
NICE TO BE WITH YOU AGAIN

THE TWO RONNIES OBE

IN A PACKED PROGRAMME TONIGHT ...

A STAR BOOK
published by
the Paperback Division of
W. H. ALLEN & Co. Ltd.

A Star Book
Published in 1978
by the Paperback Division of
W. H. Allen & Co. Ltd
A Howard and Wyndham Company
44 Hill Street, London W1X 8LB

This edition reprinted 1979

Printed in Great Britain by
The Anchor Press Ltd
Tiptree, Essex

ISBN 0 352 30204 6

FOREWORD

Can you spot what was finally used on the air
from the following pages? All the great gags
from the last series are here — but there's
more. What you've got is the rehearsal script,
just as the Ronnies had.

So make your choice, exactly as they did! And
send your attempt at producing the same
selection as the best qualified comedians in the
business (plus, in twelve words, your reasons
why the two Ronnies so richly deserve their
OBEs) to:

The Society for Silly Competitions,
38, The Street Where Dicken was Born,
The Team that Won the Cup in 1925 Park,
Queen Elizabeth Slept Here,
Sexes (anag.).

GOOD EVENING...

Ronnie Corbett: It's good to be back with you
once again, isn't it, Ronnie?

Ronnie Barker: Yes, indeed it is. And in a packed programme tonight we'll be bringing you the wonderfully evocative sound of leather striking willow — a golfer kicking a tree that's in the way.

RC: And I'll be meeting the first of a number of people with a real sense of purpose in life. This week — a man who's abolutely bent on playing the trumpet, but a perfectly good husband and father the rest of the time.

RB: But first, here is the news. The Irish Guinness shortage was solved today. From tomorrow, customers will be served with lager and sunglasses.

RC: Mr. Cyril Smith lost some of his enthusiasm for proportional representation today when his vote was taken away from him and given to his bottom.

RB: And George Mumble, the Bodmin man who swallowed two hundredweight of cascara for a bet on Coronation Night, today celebrated his Silver Jubilee. He's been on the throne for twenty-five years.

RC: Whilst a nationwide survey of British women's underwear preferences reveals that the most favoured garment is pants in Hants, stays in Hayes, knickers in Twickers and in Rockall nothing much to speak of.

RB: The Family Planning Association's weekend course for Reluctant Women has been cancelled. They've all got headaches.

RC: And news tonight of panic-buying in Scotland. There is none.

RB: And now a sketch featuring
Mr. Ronnie Corbett — whose
uncle's will was published
today. Ronnie gets a large
settlement. It's a cottage
that's falling into a quarry.

THE ARTS-
NATIONWIDE

Ronnie Corbett: .Tonight we preview three
new Swedish films —
'Hiawatha and his Minihaha',
'Hiawatha and his
Maxihaha', and 'Hiawatha
and his Bloody Enormous
Haha'.

Ronnie Barker: Then we'll be looking at the works of three distinguished poets — Gerard Manley Hopkins, Gerard Not-So-Manly Hopkins and Gerard Out-And-Out Raving Fairy Hopkins.

RC: Maybe we'll have time for a peek at the Cement Marketing Board's Sculpture Exhibition which opened in London today. The main competition was for carvings of the world's great lovers done entirely in limestone. And Casanova won by a long chalk.

RB: By the way, a large audience attended the world premiere this evening of a symphony written entirely by two newly-weds. It starts with a roll on the drums, continues with a squeeze on the harmonium and builds to a big finish on the linoleum.

RC: Earlier today, at Sotheby's, lot 36, a ton of cascara, was eaten by lot 37, an elephant. Lot 37A, a last minute surprise, failed to find a buyer.

RB:	Next week we'll be looking at three controversial paintings. Paris, seen through the eyes of a Paris artist, Madrid through the eyes of a Madrid artist and Pisa through the eyes of a Pisa artist.
RC:	And, as if that isn't enough, we'll be taking a look at the latest avant-garde New Wave porn movie. It has no beginning — just two middles and a climax.

RB: Mr. Zachariah Mole, the world's Untidiest Man, died today. His body is now lying in a state.

IT'S GOOD TO BE BACK WITH YOU ONCE AGAIN...

Ronnie Barker: Yes, indeed it is, and in a packed programme tonight we'll be examining that harsh cotton material for making jeans — denim — and wondering if it can erode our differentials.

13

Ronnie Corbett: Then I'll be demonstrating the latest cooking aid from Africa — the non-pan frying stick.

RB: But first, the news. After three years of hard work, Irish Intelligence experts today cracked Britain's Highway Code.

RC: Whilst, at home, there was consternation in Downing Street this morning when one of Denis Healey's eyebrows was indecently assaulted by a hedgehog.

RB: And trouble at Dartmoor Prison today when a bomb destroyed the toilet block. Local residents have complained that, since then, at least twenty inmates have been seen going over the wall.

RC: There was an accident on the B717 today when a cloud of locusts collided with a plague of frogs going in the other direction. Police have appealed for Jehovah's Witnesses.

RB: British Post Office Directory Enquiries operators are the politest in the world. A survey published today reveals they hardly ever answer back.

RC: *Good Housekeeping* magazine today named Elizabeth Taylor "Good Housekeeper of the Year". She's been divorced five times and always kept the house.

RB: Finally, tonight a new pub opened its doors here in Shepherds Bush. It's jointly run by Mary Whitehouse and Percy Edwards and it's called "The Prig and Whistle".

RC: But now a sketch — featuring Mr. Ronnie Barker whose hit single this week shot up to number thirty-six in the Irish Top Twenty.

VARIOUS FUNCTIONS...

Ronnie Barker: The Amalgamated Society of Not-Very-Keen Husbands and Less-Than-Enthusiastic Wives had their Annual Get-together last night.

Ronnie Corbett: Speaking today at the Weymouth W.I., an unmarried mother of three blamed her situation on the fact that she was sheltered too much when younger. First in a bus shelter, then in an old air-raid shelter, then a taxi shelter . . .

RB: The Friends of the Earth Festival at Stonehenge adjourned at one o'clock today. for brown rice and curried beans on bio-degradable plates. Fourteen Friends later re-cycled their lunches.

RC: Whilst this week's cancellations due to lack of support include — The Agoraphobia Society's Field Day, the Deeply Introspective Persons' Open Day and Eunuchs' Ladies Night.

RB: But there is a grand reunion
R.A.F. dinner at the
Connaught Rooms,
Cardington. It's for the three
thousand men who fought in
Wellingtons, the fifty-five
who did it in battered suedes
and one in pink mules.

IN A PACKED PROGRAMME TONIGHT...

Ronnie Barker:	. . . we'll be discussing four new classic series — "What Katy Did", "What Katy Did Next", "Who Did What to Katy" and "Son of Katy".
Ronnie Corbett:	And I'll be telling you about the octopus saved from drowning this week on the Argyllshire coast. A passing piper gave it the kiss of life and three choruses of "A Scottish Soldier".
RB:	But first, the news. Three hundred Irishmen fell into a ditch beside the M99 today, causing a small navvylanche.

RC: And British Rail has introduced a new passenger service. It offers you breakfast in Aberdeen, lunch in Newcastle, dinner in London and your luggage in Birmingham.

RB: A Section of Cruft's Dog Show had to be evacuated today after flooding. The dog responsible was a Great Dane named Three and a Half Litre Rover.

RC: And there was a red alert at Wormwood Scrubs this morning when it was realised that twenty-six of the prisoners had put their names down for picnic lunches.

RB: There was traffic confusion at Heathrow this morning when Raquel Welch popped into London for the day. There was total chaos later when she popped out again.

RC: An accident at a Hollywood Bowling Alley today when Telly Savalas bent to do up a shoelace. A passer-by stuck two fingers up his nostrils.

RB: Mario Wide-Boy Minelle was today arrested by the Serious Crimes Squad. He was then chased round the cells with a custard pie by the Silly Crimes Squad.

RC: In the next sketch I play the hero who bravely saves a sweet young girl from molestation — by taking a cold shower.

WOGS
BEGIN AT OXFORD STREET...

Ronnie Barker: News from Barcelona that an
English girl has been fined
twenty thousand pesetas after
taking her clothes off for a
bask. The Basque got three
months.

Ronnie Corbett:	Steve Austin, the Six Million Dollar Man, was found guilty of speeding in his bionic car in Sacramento, California, this week. The judge ordered that he be fined one thousand dollars and dismantled for three months.
RB:	And in Carcassonne, in southern France, a Great Dane has been crossed with a bicycle pump to produce a dog that really puts the wind up postmen.
RC:	His Holiness the Pope mingled informally with the crowd in St. Peter's Square today when his balcony collapsed.
RB:	And last minute fashion news. French designer Pierre Matlot has designed a bra with three cups. Fashion experts say it has a two to one chance of catching on.

Foreign news. French wine-growers fear that this year's vintage may be entirely spoiled owing to the grape treaders' sit-in.

HERE IN THE STUDIO TO TALK TO US WILL BE...

Ronnie Barker: ... Mr. Harry Laycock, the world famous emulator of Professor Higgins, who taught himself to talk to domestic animals. Now he says he is giving it up. All they ever do is go on about their operations.

Ronnie Corbett:	And we'll be introducing a talking dog who's gained something of a reputation as a sheep worrier. He runs after them and shouts "Mint Sauce! Mint Sauce!"
RB:	But first, here is the news. At the Indoor Horticultural Show today, first place in the All Comers Posy Class was taken by Mr. T.A. Rose with two bunches of pansies. Second place was taken by two pansies with a bunch of roses.

RC: Mental cruelty was held as proved in the defended divorce case of Todwick versus Todwick today. Mr. Todwick admitted his wife's accusation that he constantly brought up her poor cooking during conversation.

RB: Home Office researchers have at last determined what Scotsmen do with old razor blades. They shave with them.

RC: By the way, we've just had news from the Motoring Unit of a diversion on the A12. Drivers are being highly diverted by a lady undressing in an upstairs window just this side of Gallows Corner.

RB: And, let us remind you that the new series *Build Your Own Home* later tonight looks at jerry-built houses. Then some that are Froggy built and a few that have been chucked up by the Dagoes. But now, a sketch — featuring Mr. Ronnie Corbett, whose wife thinks he's the salt of the earth. That's why she keeps him in the cellar.

VIVE LE SPORT!

Ronnie Barker: Soccer violence. Fighting between Rovers and United fans tonight was interrupted for ninety minutes when the pitch was invaded by twenty-two players.

Ronnie Corbett: Whilst, at the combined Highland Games and Vegetable show held today, Mr. Hamish MacGillivray set a new record of 226 feet in the salad-tossing event.

TOSSING
THE
SALAD

RB: The draw for next year's Wimbledon Doubles' Championship was made tonight. There will be a confused opening round in which a woman, and a man who used to be a woman, meet a man, and a woman who used to be a man. The winners of that match will play a man who became a woman but is now a man again, partnered by a woman who's saving up to be a ballboy.

RC: And there were red faces at Wembley tonight when the new fencing turned out to be completely ineffectual. It totally failed to stop the England team from getting on the pitch.

RB: Les Grout, the only man ever to play in an all Ladies Soccer team said tonight that he was very happy after his first week with his new club. He scored three times this evening — once in the match and twice in the showers.

RC: In tonight's wrestling at Lewisham Baths, Larry Grayson beat John Inman by a technical submission. They were fighting for the Grappling Game's biggest ever purse. About that big . . . and covered with pink sequins.

RB: It was a lucky day again for Honest Jack Duhamel, the bookie cum sex maniac. He made indecent suggestions to ten girls during the 3.30 at Sandown Park — only three ran.

RC: At Crystal Palace this evening, Neville Stitch broke his own world record in the eight hundred metres. He was so pleased he went on to try the high hurdles, but, thinking they were the low hurdles, he shattered his personal best.

RB: And, by the way, later in the programme, Monsieur Pierre Bouffon, France's most amorous football manager, will tell us of his club's EUFA Cup progress and why he's always glad to get the first leg over.

AND WE'LL BE INTRODUCING YOU TO...

Ronnie Corbett: ... the clumsy owner of a fish and chip shop with a long record of wife-battering.

Ronnie Barker: But first, the news. The highlight of yesterday's Annual Corroboree of all the cannibal tribes of New Guinea was when the top came off a scantily-clad showgirl to reveal a cake.

RC: At Paddington today, the Plymouth line was subject to delay. The 11.42 was on time, the 15.29 was a little late and the 19.45 train was very late. Passengers received apologies and their demob suits.

RB: A car mounted the kerb outside Mrs. Mary Whitehouse's home this evening so she threw a bucket of water over it.

RC: Whilst Arnold Crump, a six foot nine, ham-fisted hairy drunk with a short temper, bad breath, acne, dandruff and fleas was named by Scotland Yard today as Britain's Most Unwanted Man.

RB: Meanwhile, the search for the man who terrorises nudist camps with a bacon slicer goes on. Inspector Lemuel Jones had a tip-off this morning but hopes to be back on duty tomorrow.

RC: An unhappy moment at Kings Cross station tonight when a Scottish football fan lost all his luggage moments after stepping off the train. The cork fell out.

Mr. Ronnie Corbett — he was slightly wounded whilst swimming at Torquay this summer when he was hooked and reeled in by an angler. He was then deeply mortified by being thrown back.

REGINA
v
A
KIDDERMINSTER
MAN

Ronnie Barker: The Kidderminster man who today squirted cavity wall foam up a policeman's trousers will appear in court tomorrow charged with insulating behaviour.

Ronnie Corbett: Flann O'Brien and Faustus Kelly were fined at Kilburn Magistrates' Court this morning for causing an affray. Their defence was that they were trying to separate each other.

RB: The escapologist arrested for disturbing the peace in Watford last night was today bound over for twenty-three seconds — a new world record.

RC: A man appeared at Bingley
       Magistrates Court today
       accused of stealing an
       eighteen pound tin of
       bicarbonate of soda. Police
       said that he had swallowed
       the evidence. He was
       remanded into custody
       pending very loud reports.

RB: And the driving instructor
       who undid a lady's bra whilst
       giving her a lesson, today
       had his licence endorsed for
       exceeding the limits in a
       built-up area.

RC: A man was charged at
       Henlade today with ill-
       treating his wife. She had
       apparently had so many
       silicone operations, he was
       using her to polish his car.

We had hoped to be bringing you...

Ronnie Corbett: ... the doctor who has a private practice in Bath and getting him to draw a diagram.

Ronnie Barker: But we will be reading excerpts from the book written by a man who tried to carry a refrigerator from Athens to Middlesbrough and gave himself a hernia. It's called *A Fridge Too Far*.

RC: Next week, on the other hand, we'll have a number of guests for you. Including the Tinsley man who got into the headlines when he sat on a lathe and gave himself a nasty turn.

RB: But first, the news. A teacher with special responsibility for sex education at a Manchester comprehensive school today eloped with one of his visual aids.

RC: And it was announced in London today that British Leyland have given up the old clocking-on system. Workers will now be invited to sign the Visitors' Book.

RB: Latest reports on the Electricity Board man who survived a 330,000 volt shock say that he's sitting up in his hospital bed, smiling and cheerful. He's feeding himself, two tumble driers, a dish washer, the entire lighting system and Esther Rantzen's toothbrush.

RC: Whilst in London's West End tonight, a Scotsman died of starvation on the back seat of a Pay-as-You-Leave bus.

RB: But now a sketch featuring Mr. Ronnie Corbett who recently gained a degree in mathematics from the Open University and is looking for a job as a pocket calculator.

THAT'S SHOW BUSINESS

Ronnie Corbett: Later on, Larry Grayson'll be here to tell us that his earnings as a star make it quite certain he'll never be in Normal Street again.

Ronnie Barker: And we'll have an Outside Broadcast direct from the stage where the Flying Squad are presenting their annual Drag Revue — *The Sweetie.*

RC: After which, we hope to talk to Mr. Tiny Adcock who's spent his entire working life in the circus, clearing up after the elephants. He'll be telling us how he took his first steps in the business.

RB: Then I'll be having a word to the song and dance man who yesterday put on a happy face, buttoned up his overcoat, pulled on his fancy pants and zippered his doodah.

RC: But first, two late news items. The record company who recently released Rod McKuen's Greatest Hits without a hole in the middle today offered the following advice to buyers. Take a Polo mint and, using it as a template, bore a hole through the centre of the record. For even better results, play the Polo mint.

RB: And a sad day today at Lord George Davidson's Circus. Arthur Yallop the Human Fly committed insecticide.

I'LL BE INVOLVED IN A FACE-TO-FACE CONFRONTATION WITH...

Ronnie Barker: ... the Exeter newly-weds who this week had their prayers answered for a honeymoon away from it all, with luxury yet guaranteed quiet and seclusion. British Leyland have booked them into the back'seat of a Rover that's still on the production line.

Ronnie Corbett: And we'll be talking to the woman who has just sold her Victorian brass bedstead, as she is no longer on squeaking terms with her husband.

RB: We *were* to have interviewed the star attraction of Lord George Davidson's circus — Alfredo, the Human Bomb. But we've just heard that he's gone off on holiday.

RC: But we will be talking to a man who was imprisoned in Wormwood Scrubs for his beliefs. He believed the night watchman was asleeep.

RB: But first, the news. Magda Nammepiil, Finnish sprinter, went home well-pleased today after finishing 100 laps round Helsinki stadium for Charity. So did the 100 Lapps.

RC: His Magnificence the Potentate of Abd el-Wadi returned home tonight after visiting eight other sheikhs in a strenuous round of wife-swapping parties. He now wishes to be known as the Impotentate of Abd el-Wadi.

RB: By the way, later there's a choice for you lady sports fans — either football with David Coleman, snooker with David Gasman or hanky-panky with David Milkman.

RC: The Duke of Purfleet today opened the RSPCA's spacious new headquarters in Bloomsbury. He praised its design and said that the old building was so cramped, in the end there wasn't room to swing a cat.

RB: And now a military sketch featuring Mr. Ronnie Corbett — who claims that, throughout his National Service, he was a model soldier. Sometimes he even goes back to see his little friends in Gamages.

VIVE
LA DIFFERENCE

Ronnie Corbett: Mr. Percy Tweeter, a Warminster stereo enthusiast, today celebrated 25 years of marriage. He paid tribute to his wife's high fidelity and said that although her bass had developed a wobble, she still went smoothly at three speeds and turned on at the touch of a finger.

Ronnie Barker: The marriage took place today at St. John's, Spanish Place, of Sebastian Palwin-Jones and Hermione Brown-Ferguson. It was the church's eighteenth double-barrelled shotgun wedding this year.

RC: The Fogwell twins of Knaresborough — who are both dustmen — both got married today. They both carried their brides over the thresholds of their new homes but, through force of habit, dropped most of them along the garden path.

RB: A ninety-two-year-old Wigtown man was married today to an eighteen-year-old girl. At the reception afterwards, her friends gave her a long woolly comforter and his friends gave him about two months.

RC: Peter and Margaret Nibbs, the newly married mountaineers today made an unsuccessful attempt on the north face of the Matterhorn and two successful attempts back at the hotel.

RB: Finally, a heartwarming story of coincidence. Angharad Hughes was born on the fifteenth of the month, christened on the 15th, met her husband-to-be on the 15th, married on the 15th and spent her 15-day honeymoon in room 15. Now she's run off with the Aberavon Rugby Team.

RC: Next week we'll be meeting the Runcorn woman who married a Gas Board fitter and complains that on her wedding night three of them turned up — one to estimate the job, one to do it and one to pick up the bits in the morning.

RB: And I'll be face to face with the wedding guest at an all-nude ceremony who came within an inch of being best man.
Until then . . .

*　*　*

Turville Dinge, the celebrated budgerigar impressionist died today. A few friends attended a private ceremony at which he was flushed down the lavatory.

*　*　*

You'll have the pleasure of meeting...

Ronnie Corbett: ... the Irishman who plans to cross the Atlantic on a plank when he can find one that's long enough.

Ronnie Barker: And we'll be talking to a lady window dresser and asking her why she doesn't pull the curtains ...

RC: But first, the news. The GPO today announced a new Third Class Post. It will go into operation just as soon as all pillar-boxes have been fitted with a chain to flush them with.

RB: Four girls were disqualified for cheating in the Miss Greater Manchester competition last night. They were Miss Altrincham, Miss Paddingham, Miss Pumpingham and Miss Stuffingham.

MISS PUMPINGHAM 78

RC: The International Nudist Poetry Competition was won in Helsinki today by Minus Minusson of Iceland. His Wordsworth and Keats renditions got him a place in the final, where his Longfellow proved irresistible.

RB: Good news for the unemployed. You can go places as a prune taster. About once every ten minutes.

RC: Arriving in London tonight was the somewhat confused Japanese pilot who every December the twelfth takes a sentimental journey and bombs Pearl Bailey.

RB: Finally, a police message. You're warned to be on the look out for Joseph Gomez, a Spaniard, last heard of living in Tooting, whose mother was a nun in Barcelona. A one-time flautist with a symphony orchestra, he is wanted for looting in Haifa, where he worked on a farm. The police urge people to look out for a Haifa Looting Fluting Tooting Son of a Nun from Barcelona, Part Time Ploughboy Joe.

RC: In the next sketch I play the all conquering warlord Genghis Khan.

RB: And I play his unhappy brother, Genghis Khant.

BUT FIRST, THE NEWS

Ronnie Corbett: The giant worm failed to mate at London Zoo again today. Its rear end had a headache.

Ronnie Barker: A publican in Islington last night sacked all his topless barmaids for dipping into the till.

RC: Sad news from Sir George Davidson's circus — the tattooed-all-over lady has had a face lift and it's gone and smudged all the pictures.

RB: The Under Secretary of Defence today visited army units on Salisbury Plain to explain the new cuts. He explained the duties of the new Armoured Skateboard Division and received a twenty-one bow and arrow salute.

RC: The *Irish Times* published its £20,000 prize competition crossword today. For those who don't wish to take part, the answers are on page nine.

RB: By the way, later on in the studio we'll be bringing you the Massed Mounted Bands of the Household Cavalry closely followed by the Massed Buckets of the Rhubarb Growers Association.

RC: After that we'll be meeting a Tax Inspector who'll show us how to fill in a form, followed by a foreman who'll show us how to fill in a Tax Inspector. But now a story of lust and greed in which I play the father of a beautiful girl who wants an industrial empire of her own . . .

RB: And I play the big-hearted manufacturer who gives her the works.

TODAY'S WILLS

Ronnie Barker: Worcestershire's most famous gardener, Fred Waterbutts, died this week. In his will he has asked for his ashes to be sprinkled over his beloved vegetable patch in April, lightly forked in at one ounce to the square yard.

Ronnie Corbett: And, by the terms of Lady Oenone Smith-Maggs' will, published today, her fortune will be divided between her cat and her dog. The will is to be contested by her parrot.

UNCLASSIFIED RESULTS

Ronnie Corbett: Two late football results. The Arsenal/Stoke match was abandoned. The match between Nuneaton Nancies and Farnham Fairies was very abandoned.

Ronnie Barker: Stewards tonight called off the greyhound meeting at Killarney after tests revealed that somebody had drugged the hare.

RC: Fingal MacCall, All-Caledonia Flyweight Caber Tossing Champion, made an attempt with the heavyweight caber last night. He is now in Braemar Infirmary being treated for a Highland Gathering.

RB: England's team for the World Cup was finally chosen today. It's Holland.

RC: It's Ladies' Day at Sandown Park tomorrow and Peter O'Sullivan tells us there's a jolly good bet in the 3.30 and a couple of dead certs in the 4 o'clock.

RB: The Football League have announced a new scheme for re-designing clubs' badges so that they suggest the club's name. Oxford United's badge will be an ox. Swansea will be a swan. Queen's Park will be a queen. And Notts County will have a knot. Dundee will have a cake. Chelsea will have a bun. And Luton will have a loo. Bristol City are in two minds. And Arsenal have backed out altogether.

RC: Last, an item of interest for all of us and not just sports fans — Italian archaeologists now say they know who the first spectators ever to invade the playing area were. It was a party of Irishmen who ran onto the pitch at the Coliseum to get the lions' autographs.

That's all we have time for tonight, but...

Ronnie Barker: ... here are some late items of news. Her Majesty the Queen went on a short informal walkabout today after she hit her thumb with a hammer.

Ronnie Corbett: Whilst at Hickstead today Princess Anne had three clear rounds and was then asked to leave by the landlord.

RB: In support of their salary claim, the Irish Wall of Death Riders' Association starts a go-slow today.

RC: The World Masochism Centre opened today in Edmonton. There are huge illuminated signs all over it telling you all about the wonderful things inside, but no door.

RB: Reports are coming in that aboriginals in the remotest part of Sarawak are having their first taste of Christianity. He was the Reverend J. G. Podmore of Warminster.

RC: Bad news, too, of the Gay Lib expedition to Borneo. They've been captured and made into fairy cakes.

RB: Next week we'll be having a word with the superstitious doctor who won't ever ask for a specimen on St. Swithin's Day ...

RC: And we'll be introducing two young women of leisure who last week took hours off in their garden. And looking forward to the time when they take theirs off in our garden.

But now a sketch in which a beautiful blonde takes me for a short tramp in the woods ...

RB: And me for a great layabout in the long grass.

WHATEVER WILL THEY DO NEXT?

Ronnie Corbett: Geneticists at Cambridge have crossed an elephant with a contortionist musician to get a four ton version of Andre Previn that can tickle its own ivories.

Ronnie Barker: Whilst scientists in Australia have crossed Rolf Harris with one of the Five Wise Virgins to produce a didgery don't.

RC: Then there's the man who crossed a Derby winner with a nymphomaniac to get a racing certainty.

RB: And the man from Colchester who managed to combine a retriever and a tortoise. It goes down to the shops and comes back with last week's paper.

RC: Later on, by the way, we'll meet the ghoul who crossed Dracula with a haystack to develop a vampire that sucks you through a straw.

RB: Then we'll show you the Design Centre's new combined whisky bottle and scrubbing brush. Now top surgeons can scrub up as they do the rounds of the local boozers or booze up as they do the rounds of the local scrubbers.

RC: And we'll be going over to Australia to see a skunk that has been crossed with a koala to get a Poo Bear.

RB: But, before all that, here's good news for coach drivers. Peter Pan has been successfully crossed with a travel pill to produce a boy who will never throw up.

RC: That'll be all we have time for. We'll have to leave over until next week our talk with a man who's crossed the Naughty Nineties with a Japanese airman to get a camiknicker pilot.

* * *

Solomon F. Potts, America's most persistent practical joker, was buried today. He isn't dead, it's just the neighbours getting their own back.

* * *

HERE IS THE LATE
LATE
NEWS

Ronnie Barker: Mr. Harry Spelt, who has been buying businesses all over the country, announced today that he now has 39 surgical appliance shops. He hopes very soon to make an offer for Truss House Forte.

Ronnie Corbett: Published in Dublin today were the results of the Irish Government's referendum on the closed shop. 99% voted for Wednesday afternoons.

RB: The Harrow School garlic-eating contest has been won by the same boy for the third year running. His Headmaster said today, "This definitely puts him in a class by himself."

RC: This week is "Accident Prevention Week" at Aldershot and already three hundred Army wives have signed an undertaking to have a guard in front of the fire.

RB: Mick Jagger was overwhelmed by fans at Los Angeles Airport this morning. The police linked arms to give him mouth-to-mouth resuscitation.

RC: Finally, here is a police message. Will the man who lost eight bottles of whisky at Euston station this morning please go to the Lost Property office by Platform Nine where the man who found them has just been handed in.

RB:	In next week's programme we'll be meeting the well-known Court photographer who'll be showing us some of the photos he managed to get before he was caught.
RC:	We'll also be talking to the man who bought five hundredweight of sennapods in a clearance sale.
RB:	And then we'll take time out to meet Dai Evans, inventor of the Welsh Boomerang. It doesn't come back, it sings about coming back.
RC:	And there'll be a sketch featuring the well-built Mr. Ronnie Barker. Ronnie, by the way, went out to buy himself a new overcoat this morning, tried a couple of boutiques, but found them a bit tight under the arms.

THE DAY AFTER TOMORROW'S WORLD

Ronnie Barker: British scientists do it again!
Which puts them in second
place behind French
scientists who do it again and
again.
This week, research teams
from Dunns and
MacDougalls, working
together, have produced the
self-raising hat.

Ronnie Corbett: A quite different team have finally perfected a cigarette to replace the Pill. This means that from now on, you *can* have smoke without fire.

RB: In the studio later, we'll be showing you the latest thing in digital watches. When you press the button, a little finger comes out and points to the nearest person with the right time.

RC: Then we'll meet the Professor from Imperial College with a new theory about what happens when a body is immersed in warm water — the phone rings.

RB: And, at the end of the show, here to meet you will be an ornithologist who took his hearing aid to be mended eight months ago and hasn't heard a dicky bird since.

AND I'VE JUST BEEN HANDED A PIECE OF PAPER...

Ronnie Barker: A new publishing venture was announced today. Stockbreeders' Gazette and Playboy Magazine are to get together to produce the Farmer Sutra.

Ronnie Corbett   A man who has lived for three months in the London sewers was today held by police at arm's length for questioning.

RB: The Stock Exchange man who was protesting outside No. 10 all morning clad only in a one pound note was arrested when there was a sharp drop in sterling at lunchtime.

RC: Last night at the Excelsior Ballroom, Kilburn, the Shamrock Show Band called for requests. When asked to do something Irish, they dug up the car park.

RB: And there was an incident in a Walsall topless bar tonight when a member of the Campaign for Real Ale said the beer was all right, but his waitress was flat.

RC: Next week we'll be talking to two politicians, one of whom says he wouldn't mind a bit if more women were in power. Whilst the other says he wouldn't mind a bit and doesn't care who's in power.

RB: And we'll be starting a new series, in which famous people are put in embarrassing situations. The Archbishop of Canterbury will be competing in *It's a Knockout*, Sir Kenneth Clark will introduce *Multi-Coloured Swop Shop* and Reginald Bosanquet will read the news.

RC: We'll also be meeting an order of Bionic nuns — the Little Transistors of the Poor.

RB: And we'll be bringing you a sketch in which I play three major roles.

RC: And I play one small roll, two teacakes and a very long piece of French bread.

* * *

The funeral took place in Brooklyn today of Mr. Sid Schmemann, inventor of the automatic drinks vending machine. At first, Mr. Schmemann dropped into the grave without a coffin. At the second attempt, two coffins dropped into the grave but no Mr. Schmemann. Finally, Mr. Schmemann fell in, a little earth, then fourteen coffins on top. Nobody got their money back.

* * *

A FEW TITLE-HOLDERS FROM THE RECORD BOOK OF GUINNESSES

Ronnie Corbett: It was announced tonight that the Husband of the Year has accepted the Nurse of the Year's Offer of the Month. They've gone off for the Dirty Weekend of the Century.

Ronnie Barker: Later on, we'll be going over live to Victoria Station where the World's Thinnest Man is taking his bride, the World's Thinnest Woman, off on honeymoon. They're looking forward to a rattling good time.

RC: After that, we'll be visiting the Shangri-La at Scunthorpe — Britain's Worst Nightclub — and having a word with the chucker-in.

RB: Then, here in the studio will be the World's Greatest Inverted Snob. He stands on his head so he can look up his nose at people.

RC: And there's just time to tell you that George Mumble, the Home Counties' Most Henpecked Husband died today. By the terms of his will, his ashes will be scattered all over his wife's new living-room carpet.

FINALLY, HERE AGAIN ARE THE MAIN POINTS OF THE NEWS...

Ronnie Corbett: This afternoon, Mr. Callaghan left on a tour of friendly countries. He'll be back tomorrow.

Ronnie Barker: A survey has been carried out in the House of Lords to find out what members think of their counterparts in the House of Commons. Here are the results. Lord Hailsham said "Gaol some", Lord Dewham said "Sue 'em", Lord Blackham said "Sack 'em". And Lord Langham said "Hang 'em". Lord Wadham is on holiday.

R.C: A pasty faced Bamber Gascoigne flew into London Airport this morning complaining of the effects of heavy airline food and the complete lack of any exercise on a long flight. His doctor gave him a starter for ten which worked well just after eleven-thirty.

RB: Fanny Cradock's nationwide tour got off to a great start last night when she filled the Albert Hall — and left it on at regulo 4 for three hours.

RC: The London to Brighton Motorway opened today. It has been built with strict regard to all local objections and is 923 miles long.

RB: After years of expensive and dangerous work at the site of the Titanic sinking, Irish salvage captains today raised the iceberg.

RC: In our next series, you'll be able to see a sketch featuring Mr. Ronnie Barker as a nudist who can't add up, and has to count on his friends.

RB: And we'll be meeting the beautiful masochist who, when she gets home, likes to slip into something uncomfortable.

RC: We'll also be discussing
the value of hindsight — with
a man who recently
swallowed a glass eye.

RB: Finally, though we shan't be on your screens for a while, let us remind you that the new BBC series *How to Improve Your Sex Life* goes out for the first time tonight at 11.45. And just in case you miss it, it will be repeated at twenty minute intervals throughout the night.

RC: So, it's goodnight from me.

RB: And it's goodnight at twenty
                    minute intervals from him.

BOTH: Goodbye!